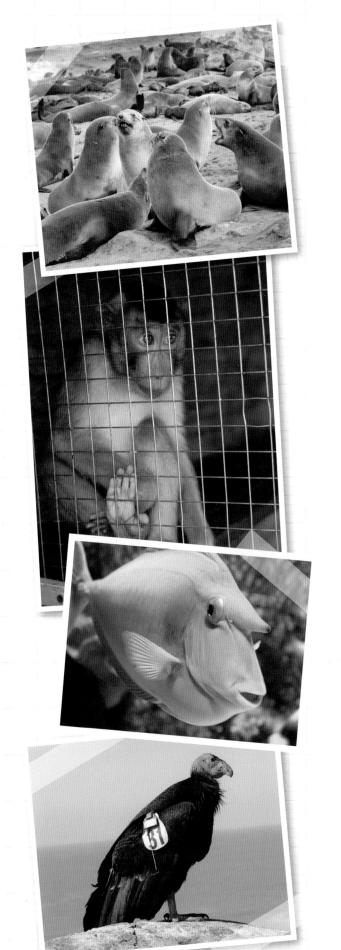

Content

WORLD OF wildlife

Almost everywhere on Earth, there is wildlife. In tropical forests, monkeys swing through giant trees. On coral reefs, colourful fish dart away from sharks. On the African grasslands, elephants watch as lions stalk zebras.

⬆The great white shark lives in the warmer waters of all the main oceans.

Orang-utans spend much of their lives in trees.

Survival everywhere

Even in the harshest conditions, wildlife survives. Among icebergs, polar bears use their warm fur coats to keep out the cold. In deserts, animals such as lizards hide away during the day to keep cool.

Elephants live in large family groups.

📷 FOCUS ON

Fossils

The remains of dead animals and plants preserved in rocks are called **fossils**. They show that over millions of years, living things change. Some die away and new ones appear. Giant dragonflies, dinosaurs, sabre-tooth cats and mammoths have all disappeared over time.

⬆Fossils help scientists to discover what wildlife was like long ago.

⟳The number of giant pandas is growing — there are now more than 2000 in the wild.

A big problem

An amazing range of animals and plants live all around our world. Some are common, such as cockroaches and rats. Some are **rare**, such as giant pandas and tigers. The main problem for this wonderful variety of wildlife is people, who are destroying areas where they live. This may cause many **species** to become **extinct**.

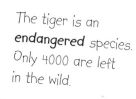

The tiger is an **endangered** species. Only 4000 are left in the wild.

People problem

Every hour, 10,000 babies are born around the world – enough to fill 20 jumbo jets! These people all need somewhere to live.

❶ *Every year, millions of houses are built on once-natural land.*

More and more

As the number of people on Earth grows, so does the amount of things we need to live. People need food, from farms or fished from the sea. We produce things such as cars, televisions and other machines, in factories. We build ever-growing cities and towns, use huge amounts of electricity and travel around the world on holiday. We are using up the world's resources, and wildlife can suffer as a result.

It's a wonder!

People need electricity, but power stations can pollute the environment.

100 years ago there were 1700 million people in the world. Today there are more than 6700 million – four times more!

Effects on nature

Around the world, wild animals and plants are squeezed into smaller areas as people cut down trees or build on their **habitats**. This leaves wildlife with fewer places to live. Plants have less space to grow, which means that animals have less to eat.

As more roads and cities are built, woodland areas become smaller.

📷 FOCUS ON

How many?

On farms worldwide, we have 1800 million sheep and goats, 1400 million cows and 1000 million pigs. The most common wild animal of similar size is the crabeater seal of Antarctica, with about 30 million.

Crabeater seals live in big groups. They feed on shrimp-like krill.

Habitats galore

You wouldn't expect to see a shark in a desert, or a dolphin on a mountain. Different animals and plants live in different natural places on Earth, called habitats. Some habitats are in more danger than others.

Different conditions

Some habitats are on land, others are in water. Land habitats may be a tropical rainforest or a mountain, a marsh or a desert. Water habitats can be very different temperatures, too — icy cold oceans or warm seas. The water can be fresh or salty.

Desert cactus plants have prickles to stop animals from eating them.

Survival

There is a huge variety of habitats. Wildlife can survive in different conditions. Over time, they have learned to feed on the food available, and their bodies have **adapted** to suit the habitat. Animals on snowy mountains, such as bears, have thick fur coats, and seabirds such as penguins have waterproof feathers and can swim.

It's a wonder!

Brine shrimps eat very tiny plants and animals.

A hot, salty lake is an extreme habitat. The water is 40°C – like a hot bath! Yet tiny creatures called brine shrimps can live there comfortably.

⊃Penguins have a thick, fatty layer of blubber under their skin to keep them warm in freezing temperatures.

The biggest loss

Habitat loss is the greatest problem for wildlife. As the world fills with more people and more towns are built, natural places where so many plants and animals thrive are lost forever.

Natural change

Habitats change naturally over time, and wildlife adapts in order to survive. In one place, heavy rain fills a valley so it becomes a new lake. Somewhere else, an earthquake cracks open the ground and makes a new valley. These changes have been happening for millions of years.

At Thingvellir, Iceland, a new valley is forming as cliffs move further apart every year.

Unnatural change

Today habitat change is different. Whole habitats are being wiped out by people — by building towns, farms, roads, shopping malls, factories and airports. Taking over a habitat means its plants and animals are lost, unless we give them somewhere else to live.

☛Airports need a lot of space, which means less space for wildlife.

📷 FOCUS ON

Tropical forests

In tropical forests it's warm all year. These places are 'hot spots' for the largest range of plants and animals. This variety of wildlife is called **biodiversity**. In the past 100 years, we have destroyed more than half of the world's tropical forests for timber and farmland because warm conditions are best for growing farm crops.

This tropical forest in Borneo was replaced by cacao trees, which are used to make chocolate.

Wht Cn U do?

Think about your own habitat. How much waste do you produce every day? Reuse toys rather than buying new ones, and recycle products such as paper and plastic. Then, fewer products have to be produced and habitats will not be destroyed by new roads and factories.

Coal is an important fuel for humans, but mining it can destroy natural areas.

SAVING wild places

Rare animals and plants can be kept in zoos and gardens. Without somewhere natural to live, they are never truly wild and free.

Somewhere to live

To save animals and plants, we must **conserve** the wild places where they live. The best way is to set aside places to be used as wildlife parks and **nature reserves**. Here, people must respect the wildlife, stay in certain areas and cause no harm.

Beavers live in rivers, and need clean water. They are easily harmed by **pollution**.

➲ People observing wildlife in nature reserves, such as wildebeest in Africa, need to make sure they cause no harm.

Wht Cn ? U do

Find out if there's a nature reserve in your area. Write a letter or send an email to find out how you can help.

Safe habitats

In a protected area, many living things, from big **predators** to tiny flowers, can thrive. More reserves and parks are set up every year.

It's a wonder!

➲ Big animals such as moose, or elk, need huge areas to to roam and feed.

Marine nature reserves help to protect wildlife such as the unicorn fish.

The world's largest nature reserve also has the longest name – Papahanaumokuakea. It covers several of the Hawaiian islands and the sea around them, in the Pacific Ocean.

Papahanaumokuakea
Marine National Monument

Northwestern Hawaiian Islands
PACIFIC OCEAN

Food for us

Grassland provides food for many creatures such as elephants, zebras and bison. However, we also need it to feed our cows, sheep and other farm animals.

Not enough room

Farms are taking over huge areas of nature. Trees are cut down, plants are **ploughed** up and wild animals are driven away. Farm crops need water, which is taken from lakes and rivers, leaving less for fish and other wildlife. Crops are sprayed with **chemicals** to kill pests such as caterpillars. These chemicals affect other animals such as birds and butterflies. People also fish in the sea. As we take more fish for us to eat, seals, dolphins and seabirds have less food.

It's a wonder!

Every minute, an area almost the size of a football pitch is changed from natural land to farmland.

⟳*Bushmeat markets are very common, especially in Africa.*

FOCUS ON

Bushmeat

In some places, people hunt wild animals, to eat themselves or sell at the market. This meat is called bushmeat. Rare creatures such as monkeys, deer and wild pigs are often hunted for bushmeat, so are in great danger of extinction.

Ways to help

Scientists are developing new kinds of **crop** that need less water and fewer chemicals to help them grow. These crops can then be grown in more areas. Fishing nets can be designed to catch only certain kinds of fish, and let other creatures go.

⟰*New kinds of crops, such as these rice plants, can grow easily in dry weather.*

Too much pollution

When harmful *substances* collect where they should not be, it is called pollution. It can range from litter in woodlands and on beaches to a giant oil spill out in the ocean.

Pollution we see

Some pollution is easily seen, such as small, factory oil spills in a river, harming fish and water plants, or a hedge covered with windblown plastic bags. People often notice these problems and, usually, we can remove them.

↻ *Some of the rubbish dumped in the sea washes up on beaches.*

If you see pollution, such as rubbish bags in bushes, tell an adult so that it can be cleaned up and won't harm wildlife.

Wht Cn ? U do

It's a wonder!

On some beaches, about one-tenth of sand grains are tiny pieces of broken plastic and other rubbish.

Waves break apart rubbish into tiny pieces, which mix with the sand on beaches.

↻ Spilled oil from tanker ships into the sea is difficult to clean up, and causes a lot of damage to wildlife.

Pollution we don't see

Much pollution is unseen. When chemicals are washed into the sea from rivers, they are spread out so we cannot see them and then they damage coral reefs and their creatures. Deep in the forest, animals can cut themselves on broken glass. At sea, turtles that usually feed on jellyfish may eat floating plastic bags.

⊃ Pollution affects wildlife. These fish may have been killed by chemicals leaking from a broken factory pipe.

WARNING! invaders!

In wild places, animals and plants live together in a natural balance. No single kind takes over. When new plants and animals are introduced to an area, it can affect the natural balance.

↪Removing water weed takes time, money and huge machines.

Introduced water **weeds** spread very fast, carried along by the river currents.

Worst water weed

Sometimes an **introduced species** of plant or animal is brought to a new home, where there is nothing to control it. It becomes a huge pest. Plants can crowd out local flowers and bushes. The water hyacinth is the world's worst water weed. It has spread from South America around the world. It grows so fast that it fills rivers and lakes. Fish die and boats cannot get through it.

Water hyacinth grows so quickly that soon you cannot see the water.

📷 FOCUS ON

Troublesome toads

Cane toads were taken from South America to Australia in the 1930s to eat beetles that were damaging crops. They survived so well that now there are too many of them. They are toxic, so when animals such as snakes and water birds eat them, they die. Local species are now becoming endangered because of this visitor.

↷Cane toads swarm across roads to find breeding ponds.

On the farm

Introduced farm animals, pets and pests cause massive damage. Sheep and cows eat grass meant for wild grazers. Introduced grey squirrels eat birds' eggs and chicks, and farm dogs upset ground-nesting birds. Local wildlife suffers as it loses its habitat and cannot **breed**. The local balance of nature is badly affected.

In France, farm cows eat grass so that there is little left for other animals.

World famous

Mountain gorillas, Siberian tigers, orang-utans, great whales and Komodo dragons are famously rare. They help us all to be aware of the need to save wildlife.

Why so famous?

Well-known animals are called 'headline species' because they make news headlines. Usually they are fierce, such as lions and eagles, or cuddly, such as giant pandas and tamarin monkeys. Headline species make people think about the dangers facing all wildlife. They encourage us to help, for example, by supporting wildlife charities. If we save their habitats, we also save all the other creatures that live there.

↻ *Tagging animals, such as this blue whale in California, USA, helps scientists to learn more about the lives of endangered animals.*

Saving wildlife

Scientists are trying to make sure that they can save these headline species. They are researching how the animals live by using **tags**, which allow scientists to watch the animals' movement from a distance. As scientists learn more about their habitats and how these animals live, they hope to help them to survive.

↻ There are only about 700 mountain gorillas left in the wild.

FOCUS ON

Red List

The 'Red List' shows the amount of threat facing rare plants and animals. Those listed as CR, Critically Endangered, are in deepest trouble. Without urgent help, they may be gone in 25 years.

Rhinos are on the Red List.

Tourists and pets

We all like to go on holiday. However, sometimes our holidays affect wildlife. Tropical forests are cut down to build holiday resorts, and wildlife is sold as pets.

❶People like to watch wildlife. Whale-watching causes little harm as long as people do not get too close.

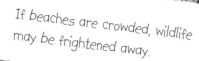
If beaches are crowded, wildlife may be frightened away.

Holiday fun

Holidays and tourism affect wildlife in different ways. As people take over beaches for sunbathing and swimming, sea turtles who used to lay their eggs in the sand may be frightened away, shellfish are often collected to sell to visitors, and noisy speedboats may scare away fish, dolphins and seals.

Support **ecotourism** if you can. This is when tourists visit places where the local wildlife is respected, cared for and disturbed as little as possible.

Wht Cn U do?

Poor pets

Pets such as monkeys, unusual snakes and rare parrots sound fun. However, they are difficult to look after and keep healthy. Also they may have been caught from the wild. Animals captured in this way suffer in cramped containers without food and water, and many die.

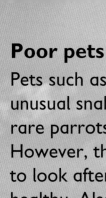

↩ In some countries, monkeys die in tiny cages while waiting to be sold.

Parrots and macaws are some of the rarest birds in the wild.

↪ To lay their eggs, sea turtles dig a hole in the sand.

Captive breeding

Some people do not like to see animals in zoos and small wildlife parks. However, for very rare creatures, living in captivity may be the only way to survive.

⊂Rare animals, such as this baby rhino, are often born and bred in captivity.

⊃Many wild animals, such as the giant panda, are bred in captivity to be released into the wild.

Last chance

Some animals are so rare and **threatened** that they cannot find partners for breeding, or safe places to live. Keeping them in captivity is their last chance. The captive animals are looked after very carefully. They are studied to find out more about their behaviour and their needs, such as food and shelter. They breed together in captivity to build up their numbers. Then some of them can be **reintroduced** into the wild.

⋔In zoos, polar bears are given food in ice blocks, so they need to make an effort to feed.

24

This Californian condor has a tag attached to its wing, so scientists can study it in the wild.

Californian condor

The huge birds of prey called Californian condors almost died out. In 1987, only 22 were left. They were captured and bred over several years, and then released. Now there are more than 300. Half of those are already back in the wild.

Back to the wild

There are many captive breeding projects around the world, trying to save a variety of animals such as as red squirrels, wolves, tigers, lizards and rhinos. If there is enough wild space and it is safe for them, they can be released. Animals may be fitted with tags, to follow where they go and see if they survive.

↻*More than 100 types of monkey are bred in zoos. This helps to increase interest in wildlife.*

Wht Cn ? U do

Find out if a nearby zoo or wildlife park breeds rare creatures. Perhaps your family or school can hold an event to raise money for them.

SUCCESS stories

Saving wildlife does not stop at keeping an animal in a zoo. It takes lots of time, effort, study, planning – and money.

Tourists can enjoy the beauty of coral reefs with special scuba diving activities.

Protected areas

There are many animals, plants and places saved by the combined efforts of people. Much of Australia's Great Barrier Reef, as well as large areas of tropical forest in Central and South America, Africa and Asia are now protected areas. Visitors can enjoy the wildlife without ruining it.

⮌ When conservation efforts increase tourism, the money made allows facilities, such as water pumps, to be improved.

Wildlife and people

Many people in the world have little food, no clean water or electricity and few comforts. These people need to see the benefits of working to preserve their local wildlife. For example, saving beautiful forests encourages tourists who will bring money into the region. Conservation is not only about saving wildlife, but also protecting people.

It's a wonder!

Black robins have been introduced to different islands, to increase their numbers.

In the 1980s, there were only five black robins of the Chatham Islands, in the Pacific Ocean, left. Now there are more than 250 birds.

HELPus!

Around the world, animals and plants are being saved by fantastic conservation efforts. Wildlife everywhere needs our help.

Many effects

Driving a car can affect polar bears and coral reefs. Burning fuels such as petrol produces **greenhouse gases**, which are the main cause of **global warming**. As temperatures rise, icebergs melt and polar bears have fewer places to rest and hunt. Coral reefs become too hot, turn white, or 'bleached', and die. To help save wildlife and habitats, we need to think carefully about what we do each day.

Planting more trees helps to reduce the greenhouse gas carbon dioxide.

*Using less fuel means less pollution and **climate change**, and saves money!*

It's a wonder!

FSC

FAIR TRADE CERTIFIED

DOLPHIN SAFE

Mountain gorillas are a threatened species because their habitats are being destroyed.

Some products carry a special logo to show that they are friendly to wildlife and the environment.

There are probably more than 25 million kinds, or species, of plant and animal in the world. About half of them live in the habitats most at risk – tropical forests.

↪ *Orang-utans are often killed in the wild by poachers, and their young are left alone.*

Orang-utans

These apes are becoming rarer every year, as their forests are chopped down for timber and cleared for farmland. They could disappear in your lifetime.

↩ *As forests disappear, male and female orang-utans meet less often to breed.*

Too late for some

We may have run out of time to save some animals and plants, and they will sadly become extinct. The Yangtze river dolphin became extinct in 2007. Scientists blame fishing, hunting and shipping for its disappearance.

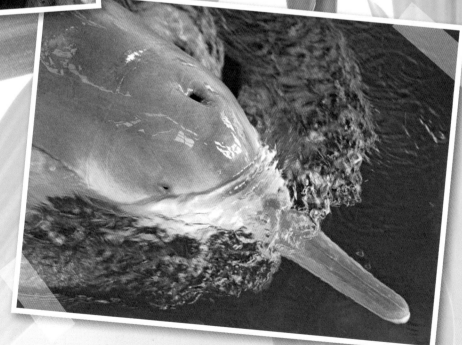

↥ *The Yangtze river dolphin, or baiji, was last seen alive in 2002.*

Glossary

Adapt To change to suit the surroundings better. For example, when a living thing develops features that help it to survive in a particular place or environment.

Biodiversity The variety of different living things found in one habitat.

Breed To reproduce or make more of a species.

Captivity When animals are contained and cared for by humans, such as in a zoo or wildlife park.

Chemical In crop sprays, a substance intended to kill certain living things, such as weeds or insect pests, that damage the crop.

Climate change Changes in the long-term weather patterns around the world due to global warming, including more extreme weather such as storms, floods and droughts.

Conserve To save living things and the natural habitats or places where they live, by protecting them against damage by people, pollution and other problems.

Coral reef A rocky area in shallow, warm seawater, providing a habitat for many different living things.

Crop A plant, such as wheat, that is grown and harvested for many purposes, including food or biofuel.

Ecotourism Tourism (visiting places on holiday) that has the least effect on the local plants, animals and habitats. It also raises money to conserve habitats and their wildlife.

Endangered When a type of living thing is under threat or at risk of extinction.

Extinct When a type of animal or plant has died out completely so that there is none left anywhere in the world.

Fossil The remains of a once-living thing that died long ago, was buried and preserved in the rocks, and turned to stone.

Global warming The worldwide rise in temperature due to increased amounts of greenhouse gases in the atmosphere (layer of air around Earth). It is mainly caused by human activities such as burning fuels.

Grassland A habitat such as the North American prairies or African savanna, where the main plants are grasses, rather than trees, bushes or other plants.

Greenhouse gas A gas that traps the Sun's heat and makes the atmosphere around the Earth warmer.

Habitat A particular kind of place where animals and plants live, such as a river, wood, desert or coral reef.

Introduced species Types of plants and animals that are taken from where they are found naturally to new places where they did not live before.

Nature reserve A place that is protected or set aside for wildlife to live freely, without being threatened by people.

Plough To turn over the soil using a large curved metal blade, before planting seeds.

Pollution When harmful substances such as chemicals or litter get into the surroundings and cause damage.

Predator An animal that hunts and kills other creatures, called prey, to eat as food.

Rare When there are very few of a particular plant or animal.

Reintroduce To breed a type of animal or plant in captivity and then put it back into a suitable wild place, hopefully to live freely and survive.

Species A type of plant or animal where the individuals look similar and breed together to produce young.

Tag A small label or radio device that is harmlessly attached to an animal, so that it can be identified and its movements followed.

Threaten To put at risk or in danger. A threatened species is at risk of becoming extinct.

Tropical forest A large area of trees growing near the Equator, where it is warm all year round. These forests are the richest and most varied places in the world for wildlife.

Weed A plant that grows where we do not want it to grow.

Index